HOW TO DRAW
ANIMALS

Barbara Soloff Levy

DOVER PUBLICATIONS, INC.
Mineola, New York

Bibliographical Note

How to Draw Animals is a new work, first published by
Dover Publications, Inc., in 2008.

International Standard Book Number

ISBN-13: 978-0-486-46893-8
ISBN-10: 0-486-46893-3

Manufactured in the United States by LSC Communications
46893314   2017
www.doverpublications.com

HOW TO DRAW
ANIMALS

2   Chick

4 Duck

Practice Page

6 Rooster

Practice Page

8 Goose

14   Leopard

Practice Page

16 Dog

18   Fox

22 Lamb

24 Cow

Practice Page

26 Deer

28 Moose

34 Giraffe

42   Rabbit

Practice Page

44 Porcupine

Practice Page

Practice Page

48 Elephant

Practice Page

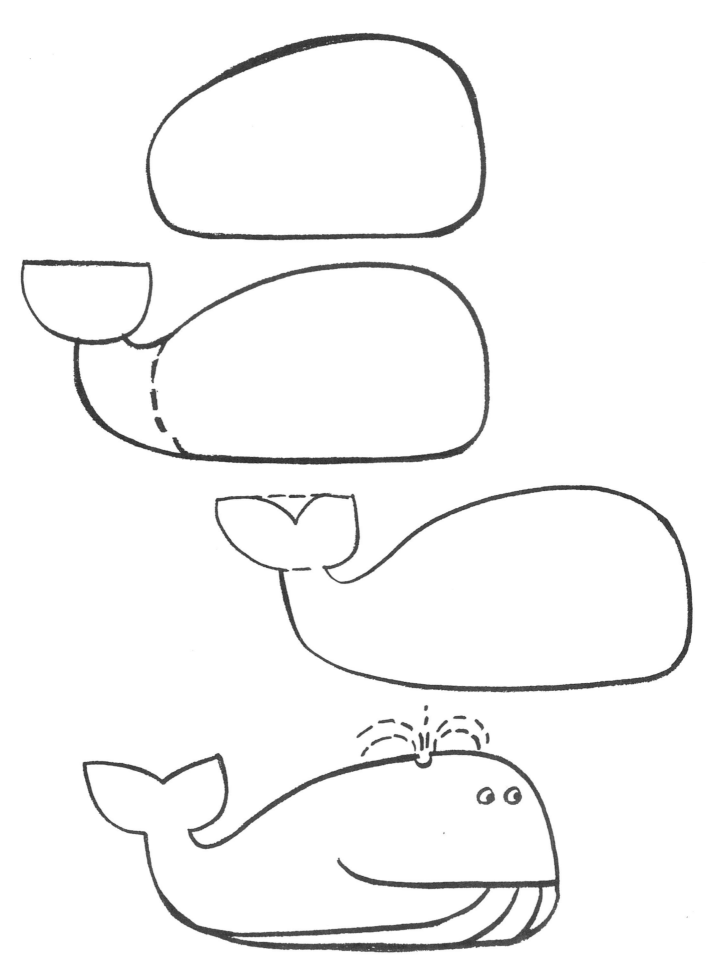

50   Whale

54 Bear

56   Panda

Practice Page

Practice Page